SUCCESSFUL WORKING ENVIRONMENTS

How to create an optimal
work environment

Written by Caroline Carlicchi
Translated by Rebecca Neal

Coaching 50MINUTES.com

YOUR WORKING ENVIRONMENT IS KEY TO YOUR EFFICIENCY

Andrew works in the design department of a factory. His office is tucked away in a corner of an old hangar. His computer regularly crashes and the light, which is not bright enough for him to read plans, forces him to constantly go back and forth to the office of the planning department, which is more functional. Adele has been working there for 15 years, in an open plan office. She cannot wait to be promoted and get a private office, which will suit her work as this needs a lot of reflection and concentration. Meanwhile, Carl does not dare to receive his clients in the dusty premises of his company.

- **Issue:** how can I improve my working environment to boost my efficiency?
- **Uses:** increase your productivity, efficiency and personal and professional wellbeing.
- **Professional context:** office life, open plan offices, relationships with colleagues, stress, effectiveness and wellbeing at work.
- **FAQs:**
  - What are the consequences of a positive working environment?
  - What are the keys to psychological wellbeing in the office?
  - How can I be at my best in the office?
  - How can I reduce stress by working on my office environment?
  - How can I use my professional environment to reinforce my self-esteem?

- What environment encourages collaboration?
- How should I balance my personal and professional life?
- How can I be more efficient by working on my office environment?
- How can I alter my environment to encourage change?
- How can the working environment reflect the values of the organisation?

In many organisations, the environment is seen first and foremost as a line on the budget to reduce. Nonetheless, some multinationals have clearly indicated their desire to improve the wellbeing of their employees by investing in ultramodern environments: in 1998 Renault opened its "Technocentre" in France, an ultramodern 410 000 m² building designed to promote collaboration between teams. In 2007 Google, which is ranked the fourth best company to work for in the world, gave the 11 000 employees at its Mountain View headquarters in California the "Googleplex", an extraordinary working environment which is perhaps even more relaxing than the employees' own homes: pool tables, gardens, bicycles, chairs for discreet napping, a wide range of sporting activities, numerous restaurants and of course pleasant and modern offices. The respective cost of these headquarters was 5.5 billion francs (at the time) and hundreds of millions of dollars of investment. But why make this decision?

These companies, whose employee numbers are constantly increasing, understood that by building a good working environment, they were indirectly showing their employees that they were contributing to the effective working of the business, while increasing overall productivity. Through the quality of their infrastructure, the Technocentre and Googleplex tell employees that they are valued and important. Furthermore, these buildings were designed based on interviews with staff in order to better respond to their needs. The environment therefore responds as well as possible to the needs of the position and above all guarantees that employees are recognised, which is the main ingredient in motivation.

Indeed, recognition is a fundamental psychological need for all of us. When this need for recognition is satisfied, we feel reassured and are free to think, organise and take action to achieve our objectives. Conversely, when we feel that we are not being recognised, we experience stress and we may feel threatened and find ourselves at an impasse, unable to think, make decisions, collaborate and move forwards.

If an organisation's working environment is unsuitable, there are still many possible initiatives that we can take on an individual level. This guide will show you how to put a more pleasant working environment in place, thereby reducing your stress levels, promoting collaboration with others and improving your productivity.

AN EFFECTIVE WORKING ENVIRONMENT: THE BASICS

WHAT IS A WORKING ENVIRONMENT?

Our working environment has a major influence on the way we feel in our day-to-day professional lives. It comprises everything that contributes to our involvement and motivation: relationships with colleagues, superiors and the different teams; the organisation and its culture; and of course the buildings, amenities and services offered to employees.

The working environment can be a source of stress in the same way as the work itself. This can take different forms: excessively noisy colleagues, a lack of light, too much dust, suffocating heat in summer and freezing cold in winter, dirty toilets, untidy office, a boss who micromanages you, etc. All this affects your performance and efficiency at work. A good working environment contributes to the wellbeing of employees, who then want to come to work and remain enthusiastic and motivated all day long. It guarantees the health and efficiency of workers, and consequently the performance of the organisation.

Conversely, an organisation which neglects the environment it offers its workers runs a serious risk of failing to meet contemporary challenges. Furthermore, a negative working environment has consequences for the health and career of employees. This is confirmed by a number of studies: a negative working environment contributes in particular to insomnia, anxiety and depression.

When we consider our working environment, there are several dimensions to focus on:

- the buildings, amenities and services offered;
- the organisation;
- ourselves and our needs;
- other people and their needs.

As such, the elements which make up the working environment are physical, organisational, psychological and social.

DID YOU KNOW?

An effective working environment allows companies to:

- safeguard health and reduce the risk of injury;
- reduce staff turnover;
- minimise absenteeism;
- reduce medical costs;
- increase confidence in the organisation;
- strengthen the self-esteem of their employees;
- boost staff productivity and efficiency.

MENTAL HEALTH COMES FIRST!

James is permanently tired. He has noticed that all his time at work is spent processing files and dealing with the endless emails pouring into his inbox. He realises that he cannot take a step back to calmly and effectively reflect on his projects,

Although the negative effects of a poor diet or the consumption of harmful substances such as fatty acids, sugar, alcohol and tobacco on our bodies are increasingly pointed out in many publications, one essential element is ignored even today: our mental health. The effective working of the brain is too often neglected, but is at the root of our wellbeing.

The neuropsychiatrist Daniel Siegel (born in 1957), of the UCLA School of Medicine in Los Angeles, and David Rock, founder of the NeuroLeadership Institute, have identified that many people are overworking their brains and drawing heavily on their mental resources, which they think are infinite:

- we try to do several things at once;
- we divide our attention;
- we overload ourselves with information.

Seven daily activities allow our brains to function optimally. They are necessary for our mental health, and each day let the brain organise itself, incorporate information, encourage creation and strengthen mental connections. An effective working environment therefore has a duty to offer employees buildings, services and amenities which allow them to carry out these activities in order to maintain an optimal lifestyle.

These activities, which are organised as different times, are as follows:

- **Focus time.** We concentrate on tasks with the aim of reaching our objectives. At this time, we form deep connections in the brain.
- **Playtime.** We give ourselves permission to be spontaneous and creative, which encourages new connections to form in the brain.
- **Connecting time.** We connect with others, ideally in person and not through online tools. This strengthens the brain's relational circuitry.
- **Physical time.** We strengthen our brains by moving.
- **Time in.** We reflect calmly and concentrate on feelings, images and thoughts, which helps our brain to incorporate information.
- **Down time.** We have no specific goal. Whether we let our minds wander or simply relax, we help our brains to recover.
- **Sleep time.** We sleep, consolidating the things we have learned and recuperating from the previous day. If sleep cannot occur in the company's building, the organisation must nonetheless ensure that its employees' workload allows them to get enough sleep.

EXTRA INFORMATION

You must avoid only doing some of these activities each day. Of course, there is no miracle dose and everyone needs different proportions of the activities, but one thing is certain: for a balanced life, each activity must

FUNDAMENTAL PSYCHOLOGICAL NEEDS

> A few months ago, Alice started work in a new position, but she does not feel comfortable in it: she is depressed and no longer takes enjoyment in anything. She has therefore decided to take on the challenge of creating a structure. Now that she is working alone on this project, she misses the time when she would chat or have a coffee break with her colleagues, etc.

Eric Berne (American psychiatrist, 1910-1970), the founder of transactional analysis, a theory of personality and communication, identified three hungers which correspond to universal fundamental psychological needs. These hungers are as important to our survival as the food we eat: it is therefore natural that we will seek to satisfy them. They are at the root of our behaviour. The first hunger appears from our very first days: stimulus hunger. Then, as we develop, stimulus hunger leads to recognition hunger. Finally, time structure hunger emerges.

- **Stimulus hunger** corresponds to our need to feel socially stimulated, to be in contact with the rest of the world through all our senses, and to avoid boredom, isolation and depression. We need to receive explanations, learn, understand, undertake varied tasks, etc.
- **Recognition hunger** corresponds to our need for social

interaction in order to feel recognised by others and by some people in particular, to receive and accept as many signs of recognition as we need to feel good, to give these signs ourselves, and to reject negative signs of recognition that we would like to do without.
- **Time structure hunger** corresponds to our need to feel framed by limits and "contracts" (definition of objectives, plans of action, roles and responsibilities, expectations, outlooks, limits, etc.) and to structure the time in our days to obtain the signs of recognition that we all need.

All the characteristics of an effective working environment feed these hungers and indirectly increase our motivation. In the opposite case, they reinforce depression, anxiety and low self-esteem.

PAY PARTICULAR ATTENTION TO VISUAL ELEMENTS

The things we perceive visually in our environment and which feed the three hungers should be given particularly careful attention, because the cells in our visual cortex are more numerous, deeper and richer than the cells in our auditory cortex. This explains the power of visualisation in sports and of visual elements in the understanding of new concepts. The environment in a company rarely encourages these visual elements to match the needs of employees. This gap is at the root of stress and a lack of motivation and creativity.

> Isabelle says that she is "extremely demanding" with regard to her colleagues' work and her own work. Her department produces high-quality work, but many colleagues want to move on after a few months. Isabelle realises that she does not share her satisfaction with her colleagues' work and that she does not give them feedback which would allow them to understand that their contribution is in line with what the company expects from them and fuel their motivation.

In our interactions with our colleagues, we seek to satisfy our recognition hunger. We therefore interact with our colleagues in a way that allows us to collect "signs of recognition", which are as necessary to us at the air that we breathe. These signs correspond to any action which involves the recognition of the other person and their existence. They can be verbal or nonverbal (a frown, a look, a touch) and are constantly exchanged in all contexts. They can be about:

- **The person that I am.** For example, "I like working with you" or "I can't stand to look at you any longer! Get out of the office!"
- **My actions.** For example, "I appreciate your work on this project" or "You handled this interaction with the client badly".

These signs can be:

- **positive** (compliment, praise, congratulations or positive appraisal, which give pleasure);
- or **negative** (negative judgements or criticisms which hurt us and make us feel devalued).

The signs of recognition

	Conditional (linked to doing)	Unconditional (linked to being)
POSITIVE	"I appreciate your work on this project."	"I like working with you."
NEGATIVE	"You handled this interaction with the client badly."	"I can't stand to look at you any longer! Get out of the office!"

The negative nature of a sign of recognition does not make it "bad" in itself: conditional (based on behaviour) negative feedback on a colleague's work can allow them to understand their mistakes and take the necessary measures to avoid making the same mistake in future.

Avoid unconditional (based on the person) negative signs of recognition, as they do not enable our interlocutors to develop their independence and leave them with nowhere to go.

To communicate a powerful positive sign of recognition:

- tell your colleague that you are going to give them feed-

back on their action;
- tell them specifically what they did well shortly after the action;
- explain to them the extent of the positive impact of their action on the organisation, on you or on your colleagues;
- leave a pause for your colleague to receive your sign of positive recognition and feel the full benefit of their action;
- encourage the colleague to stay on this track.

To communicate a negative sign of recognition:

- tell your colleague that you are going to give them feedback on their action;
- tell them specifically what they did badly shortly after the action;
- explain to them the extent of the negative impact of their action on the organisation, on you or on your colleagues;
- do this confidently and as directly as possible;
- leave a pause for your colleague to feel your sign of negative recognition and the impact of their action;
- explain to the colleague that you support them and that you value their work outside this particular situation;
- move on.

These exchanges are subject to "economic" criteria and rules based on a belief of shortage: we have been brought up to believe that the world cannot give us as many signs of positive recognition as we need. This belief has led to the development of the following "economic" rules:

- do not ask for the signs of recognition that you want;

- do not give the signs of recognition that you want to give;
- do not accept the signs of recognition that you want;
- do not reject the signs of recognition that you do not want (negative or manipulative signs of recognition);
- do not give yourself signs of recognition (positive signs of recognition).

These economic rules are specific to every individual. Some people may struggle to accept a compliment on their work, while others could feel uncomfortable giving feedback (even if it is positive) to a colleague, etc. Signs of recognition are therefore not valued in the same way by everyone and depend on the situation (time, person giving the sign, etc.).

We can also replace all these "economic" criteria by the following concessions which help us to develop our independence:

- ask for the signs of recognition that you want to receive;
- give the signs of recognition that you want to give;
- accept the signs of recognition that you want to receive;

- reject the signs of recognition that you do not want;
- give yourself positive signs of recognition.

Be careful: although it is important to know how to give yourself positive signs of recognition, this should not be the only source of these signs: for our wellbeing, we need to receive signs of recognition from other people.

AN ORGANISATION WHICH ENCOURAGES TRUST AND WELLBEING

> Chris is just starting out in a company. After a few months, he assesses his situation for the first time. Although in his previous positions he embraced the company's projects, he does not feel motivated in this new environment. He notices numerous discrepancies between the company's stated values and the behaviour of its management or the goals at work.

An organisation which encourages the trust and wellbeing of its employees above all gives meaning to the actions its employees are entrusted with. We all need meaning and to know where we are going and why. For an organisation to satisfy this need for meaning, it must clarify three essential aspects: its vision, its mission and its deeply held values.

Vision

The vision is the mark that the organisation wants to leave on the world and its history. It is the clear image of an ambitious future success, which causes its employees to support it. It answers the questions "What do you want to create in

the world?" and "What world do you want to belong to?",
and is at the root of the mission that the organisation sets
for itself.

Mission

The fundamental mission is the organisation's primary vo-
cation and its reason for existing. It defines its impact on its
environment: its customers, its suppliers, its competitors,
the legal framework, etc. The mission answers the question
"How does our work contribute to changing the world and
making our vision a reality?"

Deeply held values

An organisation has a history, a creator and a personality
which have left their mark on it, and a vision, mission and
deeply held values which are linked to these elements. The
values of the organisation represent the foundation of its
culture, its roots, what really matters. This can be, for example, responsibility towards the environment, innovation,
trust, integrity or customer satisfaction.

These values are at the root of the company's strategy
and, if they are authentic, they give meaning to the actions
of employees. Giving meaning to their professional life
is nowadays a non-negotiable demand for the majority
of workers in the labour market. When the values of the
company are shared by its employees, they ensure their
commitment, productivity and motivation.

When they are maintained over time, a company's values
can help decision-making at difficult times. They answer

the question "What is really important to carry out our mission?"

An organisation which encourages trust and wellbeing gives its employees a clear vision of its philosophy, its mission and its values. This responds to the need for meaning, for security with regard to the future and for structure, and allows a positive and efficient culture and working environment to be established.

These essential elements of the company culture can be communicated directly in seminars, interventions by superiors and posters, or be indirectly transmitted through certain behaviours by managers.

Once this foundation is defined and shared by all the members of an organisation, coherent and meaningful aims can be established on the level of each activity. The more tangible these elements are and the more everybody's energy comes together to achieve these objectives, the more successfully the organisation's mission will be accomplished. Having open discussions with employees will guarantee their involvement and the sharing of points of view on how to achieve these strategic objectives.

If the entire workforce shares the organisation's mission, this will strengthen unity and collaboration between employees, whatever their position.

TOP TIPS FOR AN EFFICIENT WORKING ENVIRONMENT

If you are the director of an organisation or an activity within an organisation, you have the following options to achieve an optimal working environment for your team.

- **To respond to the need for stimulation:** a variety of projects; development of roles; aesthetic of the building; good food in the dining facilities; etc.
- **To respond to the need for recognition:** buildings, job positions and amenities which say to colleagues: "You are important here and we are doing everything necessary to ensure that you can work optimally"; involvement of colleagues in policies through clear and motivating objectives; regular communication through the line management of the results of employees' actions; etc.
- **To respond to the need for structure:** formalisation of

contracts; organisation charts; definition of roles; time-tables; place of work; etc.

- **To vary the activities required for the brain to work effectively:** availability of rooms where employees can work without being disturbed if they need to; creation of infrastructure for sports, rest, play or meditation; balanced food options in the company restaurant; etc.
- **To respond to the need for trust and motivation:** creation of relationships of trust between employees on the same and different levels of the hierarchy; communication of positive feedback when progress is made and negative feedback in the case of failure in order to evaluate the work carried out; etc.
- **To respond to the need for meaning:** writing up and communication of the vision, mission and values of the company; coherent strategic and operational objectives; etc.

On the individual level, colleagues can act or react to put in place an efficient working environment which can satisfy:

- **the need for stimulation** (adding light, plants and personal photos, regularly switching between tasks, changing food, etc.);
- **the need for recognition, generating trust and motivation** (requesting feedback on the actions carried out, etc.);
- **the need for structure** (writing up your own job description if it does not already exist, clarifying procedures, tidying your office, implementing an efficient classification system, defining plans of action, etc.);

- **the need for the brain to work effectively** (implementing different activities on a daily basis, ensuring the quality of sleep and diet, etc.);
- **the need for meaning** (asking your manager to clarify the vision, mission and values of the company at the entity level, etc.).

FAQS

WHAT ARE THE CONSEQUENCES OF A POSITIVE WORKING ENVIRONMENT?

A good working environment is one of the key concerns of companies which want to give themselves every chance of overcoming major contemporary challenges, because it enables:

- an increase in wellbeing and self-esteem and a reduction in stress among employees, which in turn reduces absenteeism, sick leave and the associated health costs;
- improved collaboration between employees on different teams, leading to higher productivity and optimal customer service;
- a better work-life balance for employees, which contributes to greater creativity and efficiency;
- a greater ability to adapt to change;
- the understanding of the vision, mission and values of the organisation.

WHAT ARE THE KEYS TO PSYCHOLOGICAL WELLBEING IN THE OFFICE?

Below are some ideas to satisfy your needs by improving your environment. It is up to you to decide which ones you can adopt.

- Change the orientation and layout of your office to regularly vary your point of view.

- Personalise your office, for example through photos, posters, pencil boxes, plants, etc.
- Each morning, clarify your priorities for the day and carry out the actions which require the most concentration or thought first.
- Talk to your colleagues about a range of subjects, from a successful project to the last film you saw.

HOW CAN I BE AT MY BEST IN THE OFFICE?

Food

If you cannot have a balanced meal in your professional environment, ideally you should take a packed lunch and eat with your colleagues.

Activities

Here are some ideas to supplement your focus time:

- playtime (do a little dance to celebrate good news, kick a ball around during your lunch break, do puzzles);
- connecting time (make the most of your breaks to chat to your colleagues);
- physical time (make some time in your day for physical activity, ideally cardio such as jogging, powerwalking or using the cardio machines at the gym);
- time in (close your eyes for ten minutes and let your thoughts flow past without holding onto them);
- down time (relax with no other aim);
- sleep time (make sure you get enough high-quality sleep to feel good).

HOW CAN I REDUCE STRESS BY WORKING ON MY OFFICE ENVIRONMENT?

To combat stress and get out of this unpleasant state, think of these five top tips!

1. Structure: organise your office, your files and your time.
2. Breathe: take three deep breaths every time you sit down in your office.
3. Listen: develop stronger relationships in less time by really listening to other people. Ask well-targeted questions to move from "problem" to "solution" mode.
4. Give meaning. Considering each activity as unique and worthy of interest makes it more pleasant, which makes

reflection easier.

5. Get a plant! A study from the University of Technology Sydney which was initially trying to measure the reduction in pollution thanks to plants also revealed a significant decrease in stress levels when there is a plant in the office.

HOW CAN I USE MY PROFESSIONAL ENVIRONMENT TO REINFORCE MY SELF-ESTEEM?

The environment bombards us with stimuli, but also with signs of recognition. We know that we are not making the most of this, even though change is possible.

Here is an exercise to find out about your relationship with signs of recognition. Map out your profile of signs of recognition on a blank sheet of paper. In your everyday life today, determine where you fall on a scale of 1 to 100 for each of the following behaviours with regard to both positive and negative signs of recognition:

- accept

- ask for
- reject
- give
- give to yourself.

Draw a bar chart with columns going up for positive signs of recognition and down for negative signs of recognition.

Example of exchange of signs of recognition

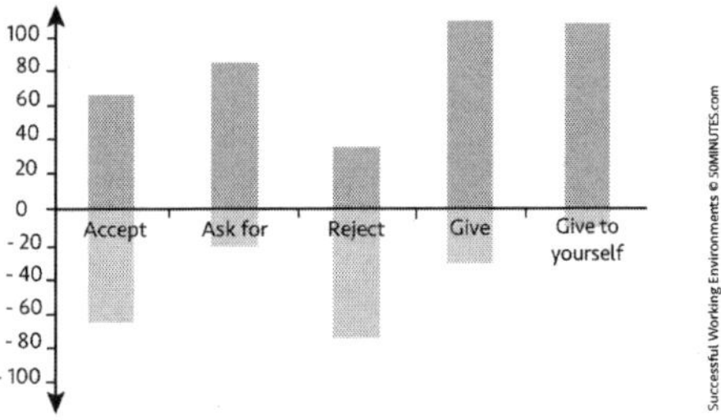

When you look at your diagram, what changes could you make to increase your wellbeing? You can note down and plan each of these actions.

WHAT ENVIRONMENT ENCOURAGES COLLABORATION?

To create an environment of trust, we can use personal elements linked to our way of being and our skills.

- Way of being: by inspiring trust, our way of being demonstrates our values, our personal ethics, the consistency between our values and ethics and our actions, our humility and our courage, but also sincerity and a desire for shared benefits.
- Skills: these demonstrate our ability, our style, our attitudes and the results that we obtain.

As human beings are consummate social animals, we naturally look for support from our peers and to belong to a group. Developing collaboration between us takes place above all through:

- the definition and communication of clear, realistic and measurable shared objectives;
- the breakdown of these objectives into a plan of action;

- the distribution of actions, taking into account each person's abilities and assets;
- the implementation of activities which strengthen relationships.

HOW SHOULD I BALANCE MY PERSONAL AND PROFESSIONAL LIFE?

The balance between personal and professional life is crucial to ensure motivation and high-quality work over the long term. However, this balance, which results from skilful combination and constant attention, is precarious.

The wheel of life

This exercise allows you to assess what part of life you are in and what realistic objectives you should set. Without thinking too much, evaluate your current situation on a scale of satisfaction from 1 to 10 and note, in the form of a circle, all the major component parts of your life that come to mind.

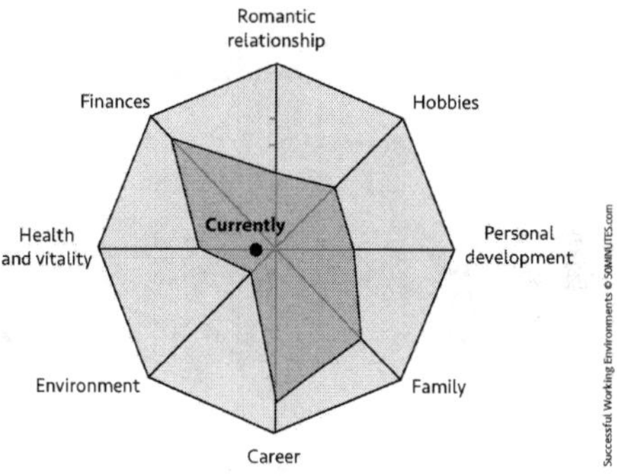

In the example wheel of life above, the person notes that on the "hobbies" side they are not satisfied. By observing this, they realise that they could get back into painting, which they stopped doing after their children were born.

The key to wellbeing lies in setting realistic objectives based on this assessment. You should therefore learn to realistically consider the time you have at your disposal on a daily basis.

Once you have formulated your objectives, you can act on your environment and redefine your horizons thanks to the many options out there to encourage work-life balance: flexible hours, part-time work, telecommuting, etc.

HOW CAN I BE MORE EFFECTIVE BY WOR-
KING ON MY OFFICE ENVIRONMENT?

Our organisation influences our productivity. If our office is a complete mess, our filing system is ineffective and our to-do list is full of non-priority tasks, we risk higher levels of stress, and consequently ineffectiveness.

To escape this state of powerlessness, we can use the principles of the Japanese 5S workplace organisation method:

- sort
- set in order
- shine
- standardise
- sustain.

The way we think also depends on organisation: if the office is noisy and colleagues are coming by and distracting you, find a quiet place and switch off your phone, emails and social media to encourage efficient and creative thinking.

Disorganisation saps our energy and capacity to think, thus stopping us from being efficient. It also impacts our wellbeing, our collaboration with others and our creativity.

HOW CAN I ALTER MY ENVIRONMENT TO
ENCOURAGE CHANGE?

We experience change and make decisions throughout our day-to-day working life. Making a decision means choosing between different possible options in order to reach an objective and effect a change.

An environment which enables effective decision-making, and therefore encourages change, gives employees the opportunity to switch off and find their personal capacity to reflect. The steps below will allow you to promote change through effective decision-making:

- find somewhere quiet and get away from your computer and phone;
- concentrate on the issue at hand;
- motivate yourself by thinking about the future, once the change has been made;
- set yourself a deadline by considering the challenge represented by this decision without apprehension;
- use a simple written decision-making tool. For example, draw up an 'Advantages' and a 'Disadvantages' column to note down your ideas in a structured way.

Flexibility also encourages change. The secret of flexibility is that it allows us to positively redefine our view of events. For example, if you feel anxious when faced with an unexpected event, change the way you look at it so that it becomes normal.

ADVICE FOR EMPLOYERS

If your organisation is oriented towards 'development' and 'training for colleagues', it is more likely to be able to overcome future challenges.

OVER TO YOU

- Use the wheel of life to take stock of where you are and where you want to be.
- Boost your psychological wellbeing in the office by:
    - adding your own personal touches: photos, paintings, books, lamp, pens... all the decorative elements that you like and that help you to be more motivated and reduce your stress at work;
    - regularly altering the layout of your office to change your point of view and energise yourself: if you can, arrange your office so that you can welcome any visitors and not be disturbed by noise, light or darkness;
    - clarifying your role and working procedures;
    - paying attention to your signs of recognition.
- Carry out activities necessary to your brain every day.
- Work on reducing your stress levels by:
    - Taking deep breaths every time you sit down in your office;
    - Listening to the people you are talking to and asking them questions to develop a realistic and positive view of events;
    - Making sure that your office is clean and tidy: keeping your office in order makes you more efficient and less stressed (you no longer need to spend hours looking for Post-it notes or an urgent file) and boosts concentration. It also influences the view other people have of you;
    - Taking care of a plant in your office: not only does a plant make your environment look nicer, but it can

also reduce stress, boost productivity, lower the noise level, make the air around you healthier and reduce absenteeism.
- Make the most of the signs of recognition that you receive and strengthen your relationship with others by giving them signs of recognition.
- Develop a way of being and a skillset that encourage collaboration based around common goals and shared plans of action.
- Be efficient by adopting the tidying system that works best for you and concentrating on it.
- Make good decisions and cultivate flexibility. Teach yourself!
- Stand up for the values of the company that you share by putting into practice small daily actions that reinforce them.
- Shape your environment as much as you can to make it correspond to the meaning that you want to give to your professional life.

We want to hear from you!
Leave a comment on your online library
and share your favourite books on social media!

FURTHER READING

BIBLIOGRAPHY

- Berne, E. (2005) *Structure et dynamique des organisations et des groupes*. Paris: Éditions d'Analyse Transactionnelle.
- Berne, E. (2016) *Games People Play: The Psychology of Human Relationships*. London: Penguin.
- Blanchard, K. and Johnson, S. (2006) *The One Minute Manager*. London: HarperCollins.
- Carlicchi, C. (2013) Le pouvoir des signes de reconnaissance. *Coaching-go*. [Online]. [Accessed 21 November 2016]. Available from: <http://blog-fr.coaching-go.com/2013/01/le-pouvoir-des-signes-de-reconnaissance/>
- Carlicchi, C. (2013). Pourquoi j'ai arrêté de donner des conseils. *Coaching-go*. [Online]. [Accessed 21 November 2016]. Available from: <http://blog-fr.coaching-go.com/2013/09/pourquoi-jai-arrete-de-donner-des-conseils/>
- Carlicchi, C. (2014) Comment trouver des solutions à mon problème. *Coaching-go*. [Online]. [Accessed 21 November 2016]. Available from: <http://blog-fr.coaching-go.com/2014/01/comment-trouver-solution-probleme/>
- Covey, S. and Merrill, R. (2008) *The Speed of Trust: The One Thing That Changes Everything*. London: Simon & Schuster UK.
- Rock, D. (2009) *Your Brain at Work: Strategies for Overcoming Distraction, Regaining Focus, and Working Smarter All Day Long*. New York: HarperCollins.

ADDITIONAL SOURCES

- Burchett, M. et al. (2010) *Greening the Great Indoors for Human Health and Wellbeing*. Sydney: University of Technology Sydney.
- Rock, D. et al. (2012) The Healthy Mind Platter. *NeuroLeadership Journal*. [Online]. Issue 4. [Accessed 21 November 2016]. Available from: <http://davidrock.net/files/02_The_Healthy_Mind_Platter_US.pdf>

IMPROVE YOUR GENERAL KNOWLEDGE

IN A BLINK OF AN EYE !

www.50minutes.com